AF575368

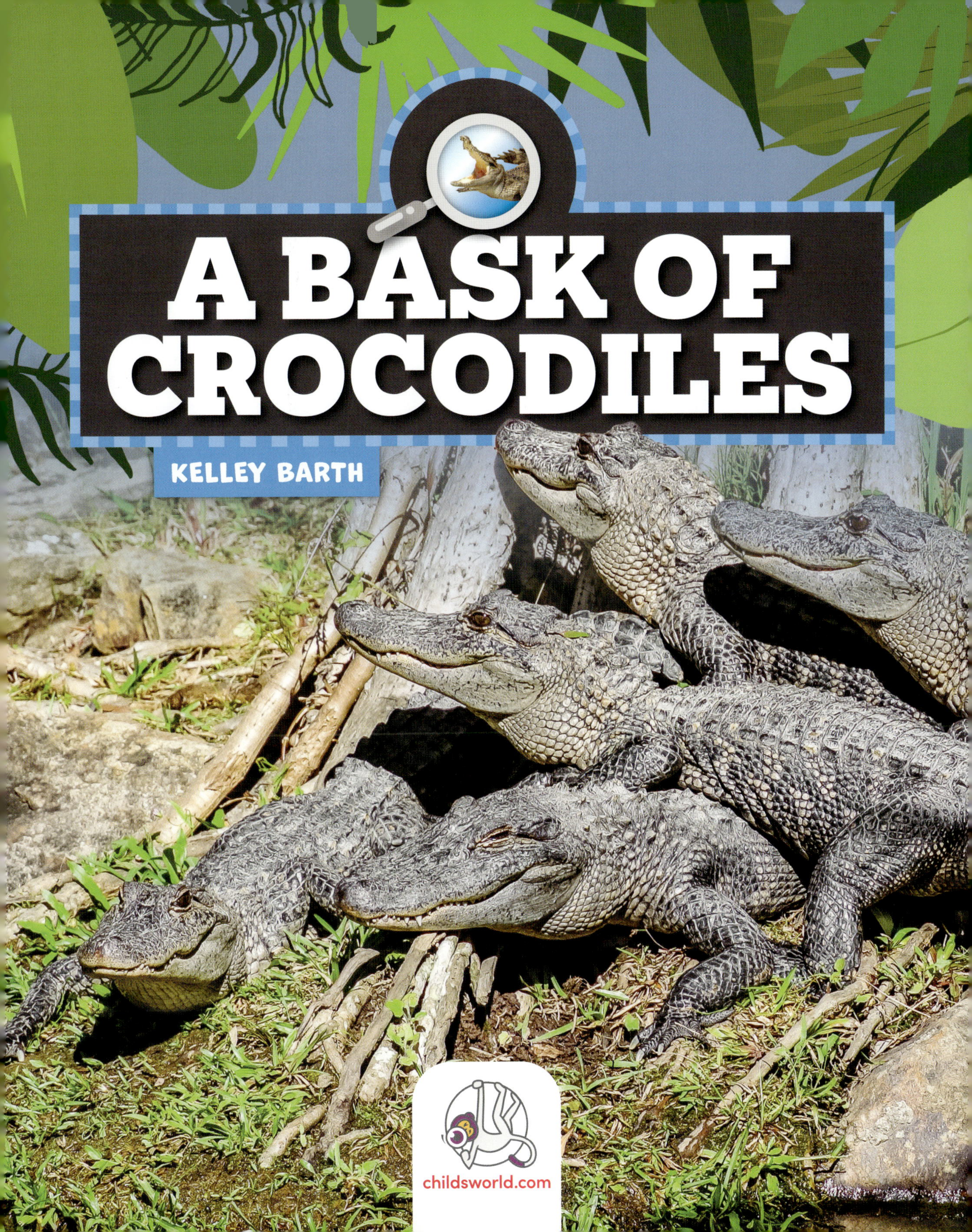
A BASK OF CROCODILES
KELLEY BARTH
childsworld.com

Published by The Child's World®
800-599-READ • www.childsworld.com

Photography Credits
page 1: ©Nicole Kwiatkowski/Shutterstock; page 1: ©Anastasiia Verych/Shutterstock; page 1: ©nattanan726/Getty Images; page 4: ©Dhaqi Ibrohim/Getty Images; page 11: ©Michel VIARD/ Getty Images; page 13: ©Ayzenstayn/Getty Images; page 15: ©Anup Shah/Getty Images; page 17: ©Ayzenstayn/Getty Images; page 18: ©Manoj Shah/Getty Images

ISBN Information
9781503885066 (Reinforced Library Binding)
9781503885790 (Portable Document Format)
9781503886438 (Online Multi-user eBook)
9781503887077 (Electronic Publication)

LCCN 2023937352

Printed in the United States of America

Kelley Barth is a former children's librarian who loves connecting with young people over stories and books. When she isn't busy writing, Kelley enjoys reading, hiking, crafting, and exploring national parks. She lives in Minnesota with her husband and dog.

TABLE OF CONTENTS

Meet the Bask

A group of baby crocodiles rests on a riverbank. Some of them play together. Others warm themselves in the sun. An eagle circles high above them, looking for its next meal. The eagle swoops down, its clawed feet reaching toward a **hatchling**. Suddenly, a large adult crocodile bursts from the water. She snaps her powerful jaws at the eagle. It changes direction quickly, flapping away from the crocodile's teeth. The mother crocodile returns to the water, keeping a watchful eye on her babies.

Young crocodiles stay close to each other for safety.

Crocodiles live in groups or pairs. A group on land is called a bask. A group in the water is called a float. Up to 30 crocodiles live together. Males and females live in basks.

There are at least 23 different kinds of crocodiles (called **crocodilians**). All crocodiles are a type of **reptile**. Reptiles have scaly skin. They are also cold-blooded. Cold-blooded animals are the same temperature as their **environment**. Groups of crocodiles lie in the sunshine to stay warm. This is called basking. Crocodiles don't sweat. To cool down, they open their mouths or get into the water.

Crocodile Size Comparison

Saltwater crocodiles are roughly 17 feet (5.18 meters) long. They weigh around 2,200 pounds (1,000 kilograms).

An adult bearded dragon is 16-24 inches (41-61 cm) long and weighs between 0.66 and 1.21 pounds (0.3–0.55 kg).

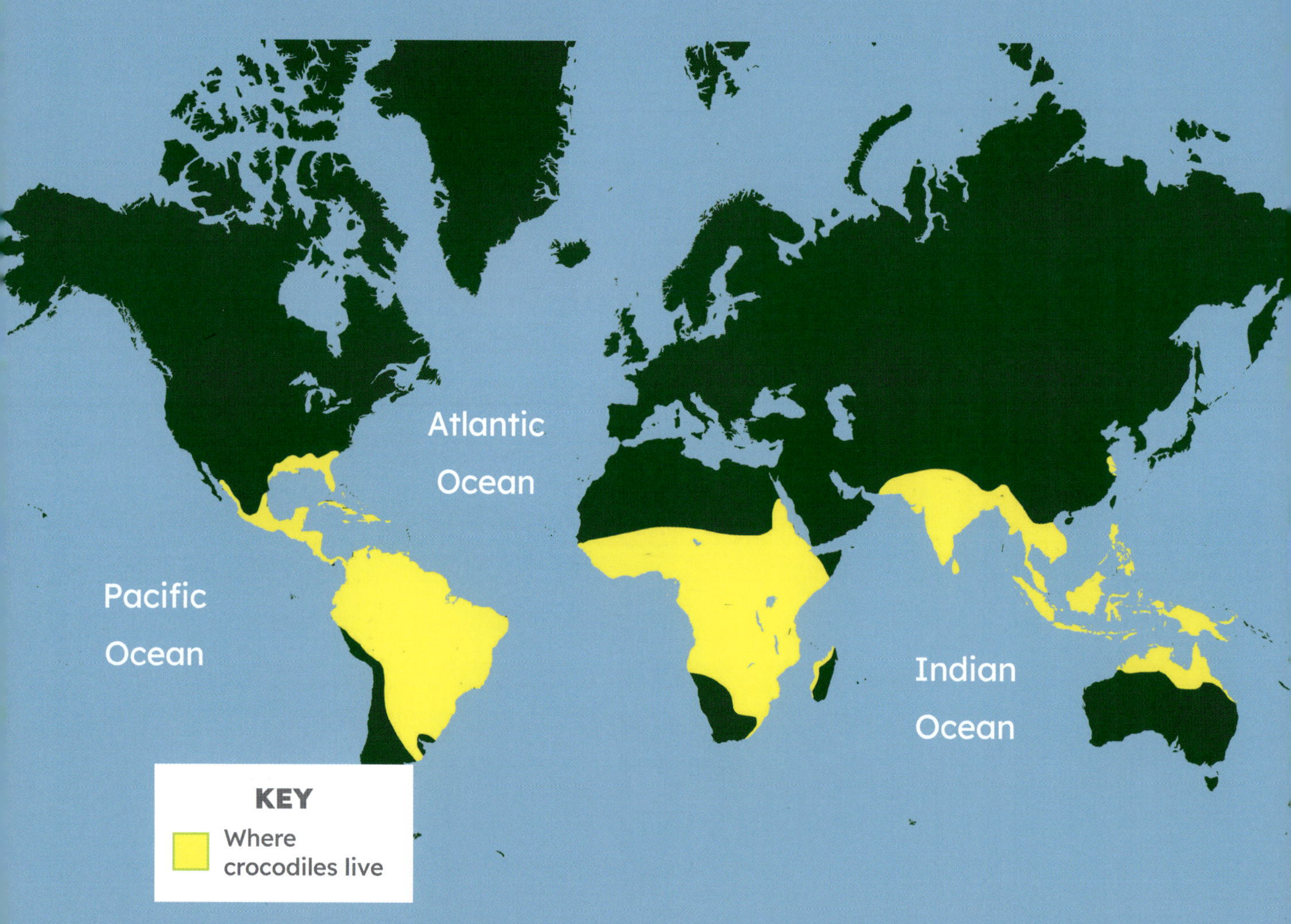
Atlantic
Ocean
Pacific
Ocean
Indian
Ocean
KEY
Where
crocodiles live

Basks of crocodiles live in warm, wet **habitats**. They live near lakes, rivers, and other wetlands. Crocodiles spend most of their time in the water. They drift close to the surface with just their backs showing. This makes them look like logs.

Crocodiles have thick, scaly skin. They use their short legs to walk and run on land. Their long tails and webbed feet help them swim. Crocodiles are known for their big jaws and pointy teeth. Crocodiles have the strongest bite in the world. These animals have been on Earth for a very long time. Their ancient relatives lived with the dinosaurs.

All in the Family

Crocodiles only **mate** once a year. When a female crocodile is ready to lay her eggs, she makes a nest. Temperature is very important in crocodile nests. The temperature of the nest decides if the babies will be male or female.

Mother crocodiles watch over the nest for about three months. Soon, the babies start to squeak from inside the egg. They are ready to hatch! Crocodile babies are called hatchlings. The mother crocodile picks up the hatchlings in her mouth. She takes them to the water. This might seem scary, but the mother crocodile is very careful.

Hatchlings cry loudly if they are in trouble. The adults in the bask come to help them.

CROC PARENTS

Crocodiles may look scary, but hatchlings are lucky—crocodiles are some of nature's best moms. Mother crocodiles are gentle caretakers. They use their powerful teeth to help hatchlings break out of their eggs. Then, they help the hatchlings find food and learn to survive on their own. One **species** of crocodile even has doting dads. The male gharial, a crocodile in India, helps raise his hatchlings. Sometimes he even carries them on his back to keep them safe.

Mother crocodiles lay up to 48 eggs in a nest. But fish, birds, and wild cats eat baby crocs. Many hatchlings do not survive for more than a year.

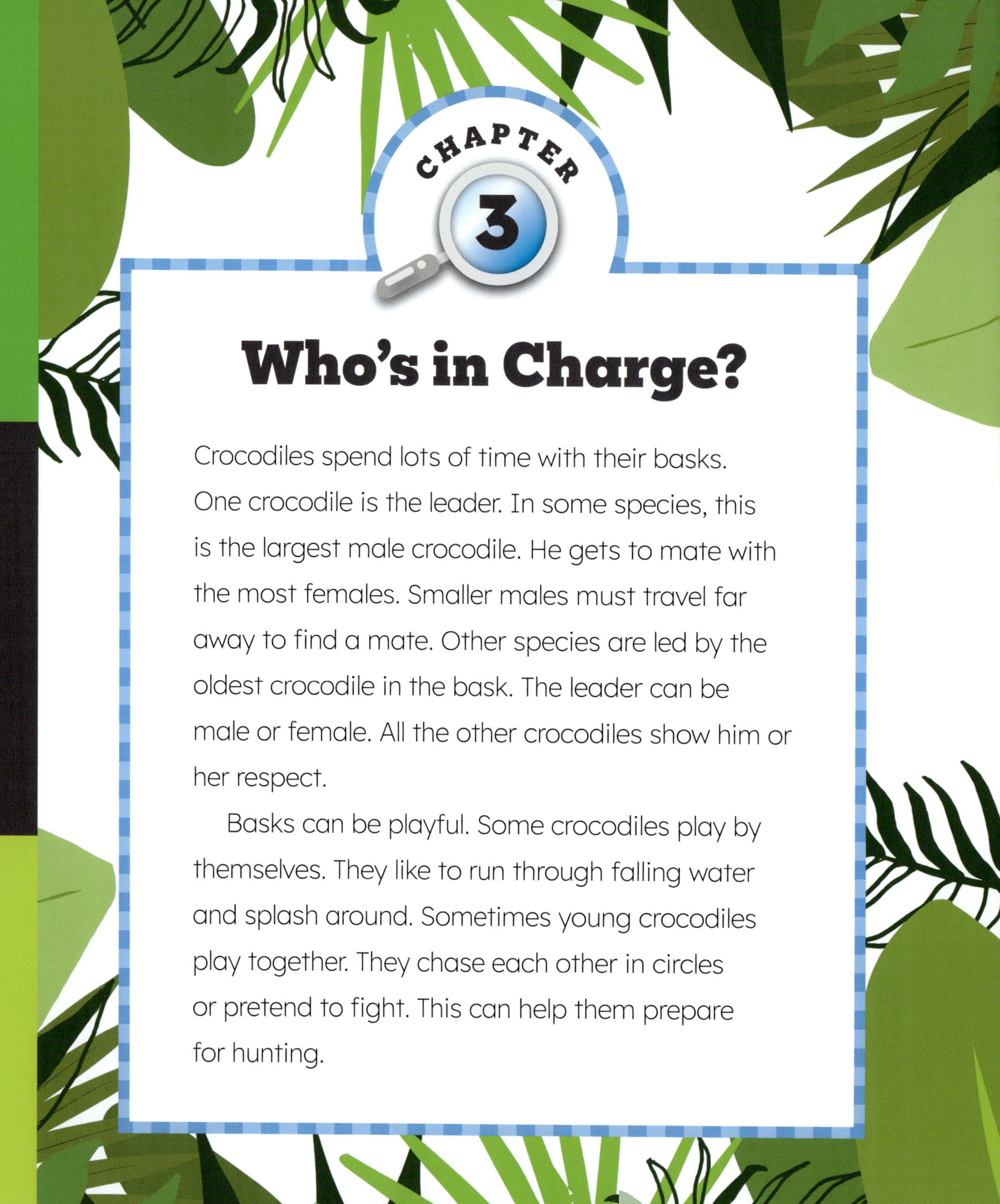

CHAPTER 3

Who's in Charge?

Crocodiles spend lots of time with their basks. One crocodile is the leader. In some species, this is the largest male crocodile. He gets to mate with the most females. Smaller males must travel far away to find a mate. Other species are led by the oldest crocodile in the bask. The leader can be male or female. All the other crocodiles show him or her respect.

Basks can be playful. Some crocodiles play by themselves. They like to run through falling water and splash around. Sometimes young crocodiles play together. They chase each other in circles or pretend to fight. This can help them prepare for hunting.

Crocodiles grow new teeth throughout their entire lives. When one tooth falls out, another replaces it.

Crocodiles are **carnivores**. They're not picky eaters. They eat fish, birds, insects, and other animals. Crocodiles are patient hunters. They sit still for a long time while they wait for **prey** to come close to the water. Then they use their strong jaws to grab the animal. Crocodiles snap their jaws shut very fast. But they cannot chew. They use their teeth to tear at the meat and swallow it whole.

Sometimes a bask of crocodiles will hunt together. One of them grabs the prey first. Then the others join in. One crocodile holds the animal while the others eat. Crocodiles don't need to eat every day. Their bodies store food. They can go months without a meal. Some crocodiles go more than a year without eating!

Wildebeests can sometimes escape small crocodiles. But they are no match for the bask's leader.

What Makes Basks Unique?

Basks like to eat large animals such as buffalo, zebras, and antelope. Crocodiles often grab their prey while the animal is drinking from a river or lake. Sometimes crocodiles drag their prey into the water. Then they pull it underwater. The crocodile starts spinning very fast while holding its prey. This is called a death roll.

Almost every species of crocodile does the death roll. Scientists have even seen babies doing it! Crocodiles often do the death roll when hunting. This can help them kill prey faster. When they catch large prey, rolling can help them tear it into smaller pieces. This makes the catch easier for the entire bask to eat.

Crocodiles can run and swim up to 20 miles (32.19 km) per hour.

CROCODILE FRIENDS

Almost all other animals are scared of crocodiles. But one bird is fearless around crocs. The Egyptian plover lives on the Nile River in Egypt. It sometimes sits directly in a crocodile's mouth and eats the leftover food from between the crocodile's teeth. Plovers also eat insects that live in the water near crocodiles. Flocks of plovers and basks of crocodiles are a common sight along rivers in Africa.

Most of a crocodile's body hides underwater as they hunt.

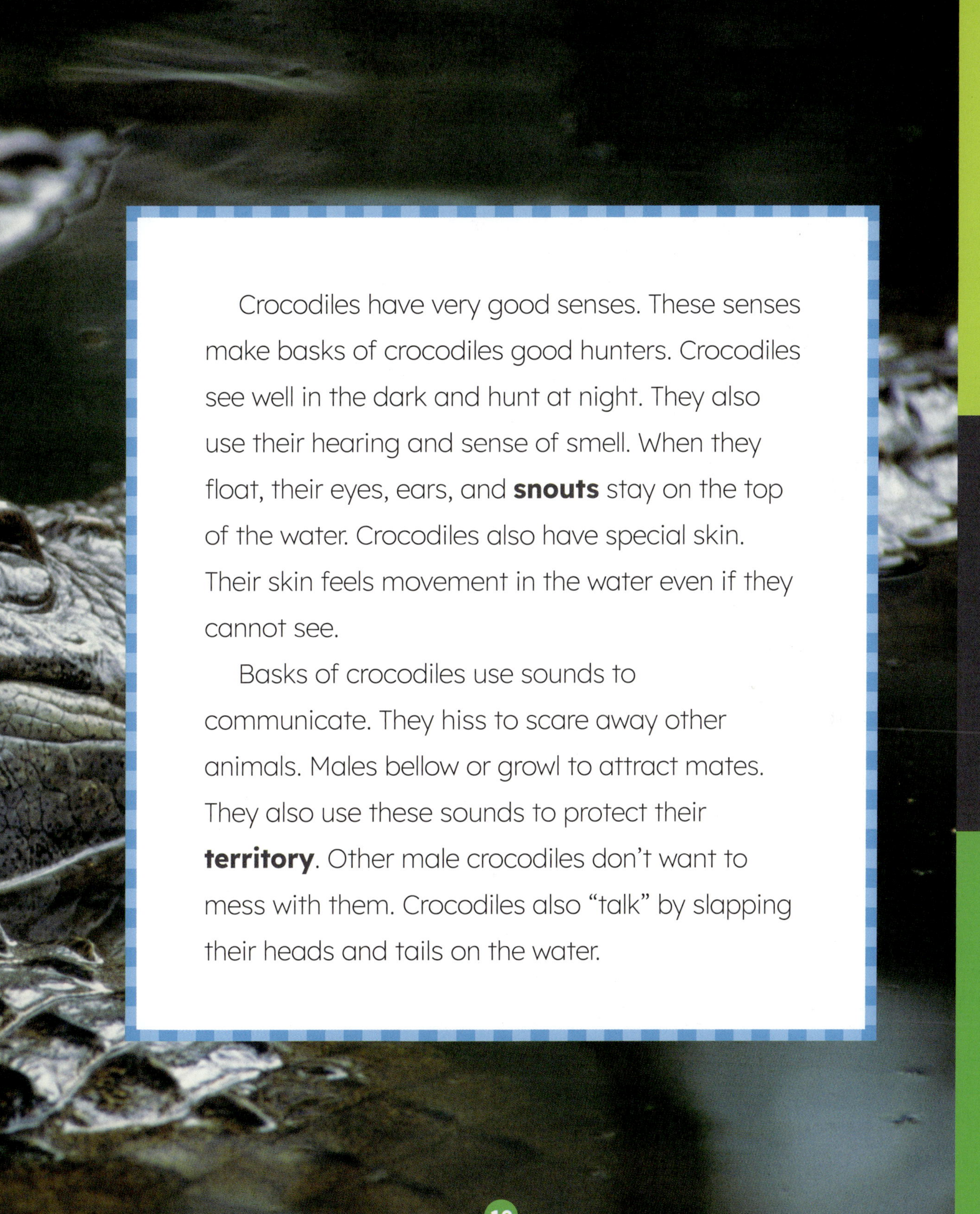

Crocodiles have very good senses. These senses make basks of crocodiles good hunters. Crocodiles see well in the dark and hunt at night. They also use their hearing and sense of smell. When they float, their eyes, ears, and **snouts** stay on the top of the water. Crocodiles also have special skin. Their skin feels movement in the water even if they cannot see.

Basks of crocodiles use sounds to communicate. They hiss to scare away other animals. Males bellow or growl to attract mates. They also use these sounds to protect their **territory**. Other male crocodiles don't want to mess with them. Crocodiles also "talk" by slapping their heads and tails on the water.

Why Basks Matter

Some scientists think crocodiles have existed for more than 240 million years. Even when the dinosaurs died, crocodiles survived. Today, some crocodiles are **endangered**. In many places, there are laws to help protect crocodiles. But people still hunt crocodiles for food and their skin. Pollution also hurts crocodiles.

A bask of crocodiles may seem scary. But they are important animals. Basks help keep wetlands healthy. By eating other animals, crocodiles keep their **ecosystem** balanced. Crocodiles work together as a group to protect their species. Hopefully, crocodile basks will be around for millions more years.

Wonder More

Wondering about New Information

What new information did you learn about crocodile basks? Write down three new facts you learned. Did this information surprise you? Why or why not?

Wondering How It Matters

Have you ever seen a bask of crocodiles before? What would you do if you saw a bask in the wild?

Wondering Why

Crocodiles have lived for millions of years. Why do you think they have survived for so long? How would the world be different without crocodiles? What can you do to help protect them?

Ways to Keep Wondering

After reading this book, what questions do you have about crocodile basks? What can you do to learn more about them?

Spot the Croc

Crocodiles look and act similar to other crocodilians. Alligators, caimans, and gharials are all crocodilians. It's time to practice your observation skills just like a scientist. Try to find the differences between these animals and see if you can "Spot the Croc."

What you Need:

- A computer with the internet
- A printer
- Paper

Steps to Take:

1. Have an adult help you print out pictures of crocodiles, alligators, caimans, and gharials.
2. Mix up the pictures on a table.
3. Sort the pictures into piles. Which pictures are of crocodiles? Which pictures are of the other crocodilians? Make a list of the differences you see between the animals. Pay attention to their size, color, snouts, and teeth.
4. Try quizzing your friends. See if they can "Spot the Croc!"

Glossary

carnivore (KAR-nuh-vor) A carnivore is an animal that eats meat.

crocodilians (krok-uh-DILL-ee-uns) Crocodilians are a group of reptiles that includes crocodiles, alligators, caimans, and gharials.

ecosystem (EE-koh-sis-tem) An ecosystem is a community of living things and their environment functioning as a unit.

endangered (en-DAYN-jurd) Endangered animals are those who are at risk of dying out.

environment (in-VY-urn-ment) The environment is the natural world that surrounds an animal, plant, or person.

habitat (HA-buh-tat) A habitat is the place where a plant or animal normally lives.

hatchling (HACH-ling) A hatchling is a baby crocodile, or any animal that just hatched from an egg.

mate (MAYT) When animals mate, they join together to produce offspring.

prey (PRAY) Prey are animals that are hunted or eaten by another animal.

reptile (REP-tyl) A reptile is a cold-blooded animal that breathes air and is covered in scales.

snout (SNAHWT) The snout is the nose and mouth of an animal that sticks out from its face.

species (SPEE-sheez) A species is a group of living things that are able to reproduce.

territory (TAYR-ih-tor-ee) Territory is the physical area that an animal or group lives on or defends.

Find Out More

In the Library

Davey, Owen. *Curious About Crocodiles.* London, UK: Flying Eye Books, 2021.

Feldman, Thea. *Alligators and Crocodiles Can't Chew!: And Other Amazing Facts.* New York, NY: Simon Spotlight, 2021.

Heos, Bridget. *Just Like Us! Crocs.* Boston, MA: Houghton Mifflin Harcourt, 2019.

On the Web

Visit our website for links about crocodile basks:
childsworld.com/links

Note to Parents, Caregivers, Teachers, and Librarians: We routinely verify our web links to make sure they are safe and active sites. So encourage your readers to check them out!

Index